THE CREATIVE PROJECT MANAGER

Brace for IMPACT!

Dr Savi S Arora, PGDMS, MBA, PhD

Knowledge Hemispheres Limited

Find more Best Practice Management Guides at: www.Savileaders.com (Example is Leadership)

To my Family for all their support and encouragement...
Just write it!

Today there is an increasing tide of books focusing on helping you attain a Project Management accreditation. However, how many of these books actually help you with typical daily challenges, like lobbying for support or collaborating in an arena of competing resources and political stances?

For non-Star Trek fans, Captain Kirk is often seen at the helm of the starship Enterprise. He'd often call his chief engineer, Scotty, for more power within a 30 second timeframe of criticality, especially when encountering the threat of a not so friendly Alien. Therefore, establishing confidence of getting through those 30 seconds given to Captain Kirk by Scotty to help the team out of a fix or disaster on the horizon is always key to each episode.

Taking an IMPACT approach will help you navigate the course of your starship's mission to not hit an asteroid but to build on avoiding the cluster of adjacent rocks or destructive laser beams heading your way. You'll need a tool kit at hand with a range of techniques that will enable you to negotiate a successful landing on solid ground.

DR SAVI ARORA

Contents

How This Guide will Help you

This book will help you via tools and techniques to assure your project challenge. The aim is to enhance you and your team skills through being:

Idealist and having an optimistic outlook

Motivational for team management
Performance orientated with perseverance and a belief to succeed
Adaptive to the change challenge ahead
Communicative to develop lobbying and collaboration
Technically briefed and reliant on realistic options.

Making a positive IMPACT in all you do via proven examples.

Each chapter builds on common terms and transformational strategies. The aim is to turn you into a savvy leader that is respected and can offer your client or business challenge the confidence to deliver. Let us also not forget with lots of real-world examples of proof that this approach will work.

Introduction

There are many project management skills that will enhance your performance. For example: How to present effectively, being a great chair of meetings, coaching team members, professional engagement with colleagues, together with understanding and managing change, just to name a few.

Starting a project or even being at different and sometimes difficult stages can be daunting, but there are several things you can do to make a real impact, especially from the outset.

Firstly, set clear goals, i.e, define your project's purpose, goals, and expected outcomes. This will help you stay focused and both measure and share progress effectively.

Keep a look out for asteroids:

Take the time to research your project thoroughly, including the needs of your target audience, the resources you'll need, and potential roadblocks or clusters of orbital rocks. Create a comprehensive plan that outlines each step of the project. Where are those thrusters when you need them?

Build a team:

Collaborate with others who share your vision, and enlist the help of experts in areas where you lack expertise. Building a strong team will increase your chances of success. Not too many Star Trek red shirts (code for dispensable crew members!)

Take action:

Begin executing your plan as soon as possible. Start with the most critical tasks and prioritise your time and resources accordingly.

Communicate and network:

Share your project with others and seek feedback and support. Engage with your community, build partnerships, and leverage the power of social media and other platforms to raise awareness about your project.

Adapt and iterate:

Remain flexible and willing to adapt and jointly improve your plan as needed with constructive, not critical and destructive feedback - you'll know the difference! Continuously evaluate your progress and make adjustments as necessary to achieve your goals. Ask yourself the question, 'what does success or good look like and from whose perspective?'. Sure, you can perform an early stakeholder analysis but it shouldn't just be an exercise; remember, such analysis is not static and will need to be iterated in line with organisational movement.

IMPACT - a framework to support your success based on real world experience

The IMPACT framework can help you monitor targets, performance and achieve success for both yourself and your team.

Brace for IMPACT

The Creative Project Manager

MARS!

I'm a Spaceman

When we take on projects often we have a set time to deliver. This element of time can be interpreted as a heart beat. The reality with humans is that when your time is unpredictably up, it's up! In comparison, with some projects, we can attempt to negotiate reasonable change, building on structured empathy and justified reasoning. Typically, more time, resources and inevitably costs will need to be addressed. Sometimes change can also be driven by resistance to new methods or the timing is simply not right.

Heading to The Moon, Mars and Back

Let's use a space analogy to portray how the environment of a project plays a crucial role by considering how a project's environment is also important. Take, for example, a dust storm on a project site based on the surface of Mars. This storm has the potential to damage equipment and prevent any resources from performing to set schedules. One could argue that this could've been addressed in the initial and ongoing risk analysis. However, forecasts are simply estimates and damage can often be underestimated.

In the 2015 film The Martian, based on the book by Andy Weir. An astronaut / explorer is left stranded on the surface of Mars. One of the main attributes demonstrated to assure his survival was his ability to perform with an attitude of persistence and perseverance, adapting equipment with the perspective that at some stage there is hope on the horizon for a future rescue.

The same is true of the Apollo 13 mission. Famously described by NASA as a 'successful failure'. On April 13, 1970, an explosion in one of the oxygen tanks on Apollo 13 caused the spacecraft to lose power, oxygen and water. The three astronauts on board - Jim Lovell, Jack Swigert, and Fred Haise were forced to abandon their plans to land on the moon and instead focus on getting back to Earth alive.

Fitting a square head into a round hole

Through the collective efforts of NASA engineers and the Apollo 13 crew, a series of creative and ingenious solutions were devised to overcome the challenges and safely return the astronauts home. These included using the lunar module as a "lifeboat," rationing power and water, and making critical repairs to the spacecraft's systems.

Despite the setbacks, the successful return of the Apollo 13 crew was a testament to the bravery, ingenuity, and determination of everyone involved in the mission. The mission almost ended in complete and utter disaster. However, despite the astronauts never making it to the moon's surface, their very survival serves as a testament to the human spirit and their acumen in times of crisis.

> *"Good leadership, initiative, to think outside of the box. When things go wrong, how do we repair them? Those were the three things that were absolutely necessary,"* - Apollo 13 Commander Jim Lovell Jr.

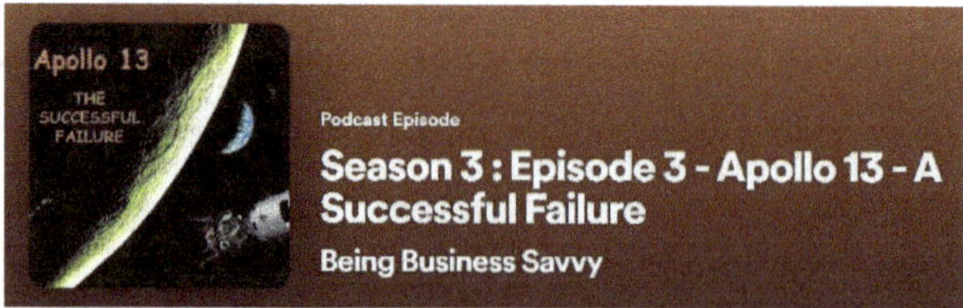

For more insights we recommend Season 3, Episode 3 of the Being Business Savvy Podcast, entitled: Apollo 13, A successful failure - available on all popular streaming channels. The episode outlines how innovation can be realised through collaboration, lateral thinking and applying effective agile techniques.

What's the difference between being creative and innovative?

Both are related but distinct concepts. Creativity is the ability to generate new and original ideas or concepts. It involves using imagination and divergent thinking to come up with something new and unique.

Innovation is the implementation of creative ideas to bring about a positive change or improvement. It involves taking a creative idea and turning it into something tangible, such as a product, service, or process.

In other words, creativity is about coming up with ideas, while innovation is about executing the ideas to create value. Creativity is a necessary but not sufficient condition for innovation. To be innovative, one needs to be able to take creative ideas and turn them into something that can be used or experienced by others.

Overall, creativity and innovation are important for both progress and growth in various fields, including science, technology, art, and business. Successful individuals and organisations are often those that combine creativity and innovation to create something new and valuable.

Its all In the detail

In terms of why the term 'creative' has been used for this book, the emphasis is on developing a fresh and new perspective using a simple approach that is detailed below. Use the framework as a guide to help you in staying grounded, respecting your team and ensuring you take the project in the direction that will ensure success for all.

In the following chapters, each of the key and core competencies shown below will guide you to become an effective project manager.

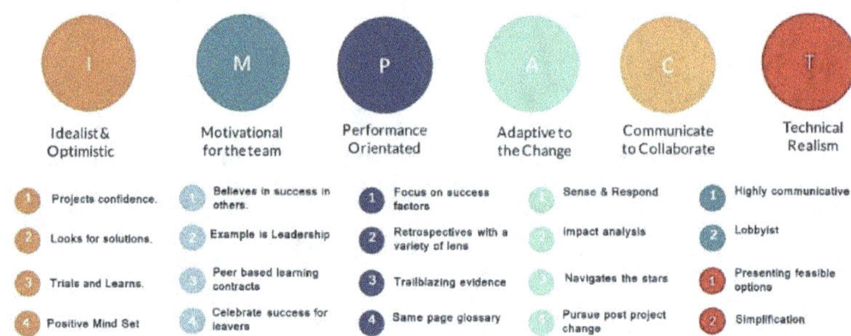

Brace for IMPACT
I
M
P
A
C
T
Idealist & Optimistic
Motivational for the team
Performance Orientated
Adaptive to the Change
Communicate to Collaborate
Technical Realism
1 Projects confidence.
2 Looks for solutions.
3 Trials and Learns.
4 Positive Mind Set
Believes in success in others.
Example is Leadership
Peer based learning contracts
Celebrate success for leavers
1 Focus on success factors
2 Retrospectives with a variety of lens
3 Trailblazing evidence
4 Same page glossary
Sense & Respond
impact analysis
Navigates the stars
Pursue post project change
1 Highly communicative
2 Lobbyist
1 Presenting feasible options
2 Simplification

Why is Impact important?

The acroymn IMPACT should not be considered as just another framework. Instead it is a structure to impart good working practices and a handy reminder of complementary techniques when dealing with challenging project situations. However, artificial project management situations such as the US and UK Apprentice television series, the position and appointment of a project manager for each task is considered as putting that person at risk. The success or failure of the task in these programmes is laid firmly at the door of this person. Arguments in the simulated boardroom often result in allocating blame. This is an injustice to the role of a respected project manager. The show itself is highly edited with tropes of aggressive managers / CEOs being applauded!

The Trouble with Project Methodologies

Here's a perspective on the typical constraints arising from too much focus on a project methodology:

Industry specific approaches exist, and generic approaches don't always 'fit the bill' or end in successful project desires/targets/outcomes.

There is often too much complexity involving phases and stages, resulting in confusion when trying to understand the difference between a programme and a project.

Timing is given too much priority and often a project methodology can restrict access to proposing less complex solutions.

Methodologies tend to be too focused on process rather than outcomes, with a backdrop of not being adaptive enough in a dynamic business environment.

Team constraints can result from the lack of gateway/touch/checkpoints.

Idealist and optimistic

When no-one else can understand me, When everything I do is wrong, You give me hope and consolation, You give me strength to carry on - Elvis Presley - Songwriter: Baker Knight - © Sony/ATV Music Publishing LLC, Universal Music Publishing Group, Warner Chappell Music, Inc

Idealism and Optimism are related concepts, but they are not the same thing, and they do not always go hand in hand. Idealism is a philosophical belief that emphasises the importance of ideas, principles, and values. Idealists tend to believe that the world can be improved through the pursuit of moral and ethical ideals, such as justice, equality and freedom.

Comparing Optimism and an Idealist Attitude

Optimism, on the other hand, is a positive outlook on life that emphasises the possibility of good outcomes and the belief that things will generally turn out well.

Idealists may be optimistic about the possibility of achieving their ideals, but it is also possible for idealists to be pessimistic about the current state of the world and the challenges that stand in the way of achieving their goals.

Similarly, it is possible for someone to be optimistic without being idealistic, focusing on positive outcomes without necessarily believing in the importance of moral or ethical principles.

Alluding Project Confidence

From a Project Manager's perspective they have to sell an outward view of an optimist, building confidence in stakeholders and instilling belief in the team.

Project confidence is crucial for a project manager as it helps build trust and credibility with stakeholders and team members.

A project manager can build confidence by setting clear goals and expectations for the project. This helps team members understand what is expected of them and what they are working towards.

- Effective communication is key to building confidence in a project. A project manager can use creative communication techniques such as visual aids, storytelling, and gamification to engage stakeholders and keep them informed about project progress.
- A project manager can build confidence by creating a positive team culture that promotes collaboration, innovation, and open communication. This helps team members feel empowered and motivated to contribute their best work.
- Confidence can be demonstrated by taking calculated risks and being willing to try new approaches or technologies. This shows stakeholders and team members that a project is dynamic and adaptable to changing circumstances.
- Celebrating successes, even small ones, can help build confidence and momentum for the project. A project manager can use creative ways to recognize team members' contributions, such as creating a project-themed trophy or hosting a themed celebration.

In summary, a project manager can allude project confidence in a creative way by establishing clear goals, communicating effectively, fostering a positive team culture, taking calculated risks, and celebrating successes.

In search of solutions

Lateral thinking is a good way to strive for solutions typically during project roadblocks. Thinking 'outside of the box' or drawing on analogies can be a simple way to introduce new perspectives. Later in this book we discuss the art of simplification. However, in this chapter we're going to consider the concept of building confidence aka proofing using a step-by-step approach.

Let us first look at a real world example. At a leading Information Technology (IT) standards and education organisation an initiative was established to develop an IT skills passport. The aim was to help bridge the digital divide between older citizens and increasing demands of companies to use online services.

The proposed solution was to develop an online course and quiz. The results of the quiz would need to be uploaded to a website to create a certificate for the learner. This would involve data transfer as well as verification of the actual user.

Dividing the approach into a number of initiatives contributed to successful project delivery. Here are some of the methods successfully deployed:

- **Establish an interface trial:**
  Consider simple tests to assure the viability of security protocols. For example, a traffic light
  code system for diagrams to verify technical pathways between all project parties.
- **Build a proof of concept in a controlled environment:**
  To simplify the principles and baseline components needed
- **Agree standards in terms of terminology and concepts:**
  See later chapters on the importance of an agreed Taxonomy

- **Focus on simplicity by developing a list scalable components:** This will help to check capacity and future proofing for solution expansion.
- **Run feasibility workshops:** Agree the change management process and manual simulations of concepts or process based analysis.

Trials and Tribulations

In the previous chapter we considered taking a proof of concept approach. This helps to reduce risk from the outset of a project, especially if the solution is pioneering or reliant on adapting existing environments.

Interestingly the term, 'trials and tribulations' refers to the test of one's patience or endurance. That's often the stance of a project manager in comparison to a stakeholder who is often keener on progress at pace, especially at the start of a project. Selling a trial approach can also be a challenge.

The basis of a trial should be supported with the mindset of 'the art of the possible'. Simulations can be manually developed at project workshops, but actually seeing a model in operation, albeit a scaled down version, can really support visualisation of the end solution. In addition, any risk averse project members (typically stakeholders on project boards) can be more informed of their decisions. In addition, if a trial is 'sold' on the basis of long term efficiencies, this stance can also help.

It's important to consider that trials do not have to be focused on physical proofing. Understanding the analytics expected can be considered in light of true usefulness.

Real world Case Study

Let's consider another example. An organisation wishes to change its Intranet (internal web site) that contains key employee information. Sadly, the challenge is that most of the useful information is located in hard-coded (hidden!) pdf look-up files. Content owners are department based and the organisations corporate communication department are the custodians of the website, controlling branding and publishing standards.

NB Such a project can be highly political as resources could be limited to assure content consistency. To manage expectations, the following approach could be adopted:

- **Develop and share a Plan on a page (PoaP)**
  Comprehensive plan view for senior stakeholders
- **Establish stages that are easy to articulate**
  In terms of stage purpose
- **Assemble a draft survey**
  Provide understanding of the scale of the problem
- **Consider borrowing conceptualisation**
  From existing Out of the Box (OOTB) templates
- **Engage, (subject to budget and politics!) the use of a 3rd party**
  To help with best practice sharing
- **Run scoping session to sign-off architectural design and final ownership**
  include show and tell sessions to establish stakeholder buy in and feedback
- **Engage early with Operational Readiness planning teams**
  To ensure support arrangements as early as possible.

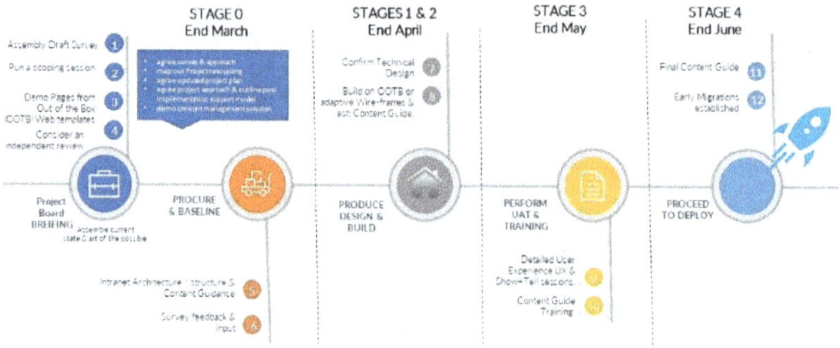

A Positive Mindset

A positive mindset helps project managers stay focused on the end goal, even in the face of obstacles and setbacks. By keeping the bigger picture in mind, project managers can motivate their team to work towards a shared vision.

> *A positive attitude will have positive results because attitudes are contagious -* Zig Ziglar - *American author and motivational speaker.*

In project status reports, it is recommended that time is spent mapping to the original plan the expected outcome over the next 2 weeks. Use the subheading, 'Outlook' to impart your message:

- What will be achieved in the next 2 weeks vs the original plan?
- Highlight a member of the team and showcase their work
- Consider that a project status report is not about the project manager but about the project team members and impact on the stakeholders.
- Foster collaboration to not only boost productivity but also facilitate building stronger relationships among team members.
- Set expectations by suggesting what good will look like

Summary

All of these approaches contribute towards a collaborative team environment portrayed by the Project manager. These approaches will impact your team & subtly make you shine too!

Its all about keeping the mission and journey alive in the dreams of the team and stakeholders expectations. They best you can do is demonstrate the art of the possible with quick wins and steady confidence inducing plans.

Example is Leadership - Albert Schweitzer

In the next chapter we cover celebrating successes in more detail, i.e: no matter how small the win, this helps build momentum and motivation for continued progress.

SPACEX

Motivational for the team

> *'Project management is like juggling three balls – time, cost and quality. Program management is like a troupe of circus performers standing in a circle, each juggling three balls and swapping balls from time to time.' - G. Reiss*

Regardless of the semantics of the leadership role, the most immediate requirement is to show that you're in control and you can champion the given cause. In some cases, if senior stakeholders or sponsors lose faith in the leadership of the programme, the manager may even be side-lined.

Believes in the Success of Others & The Journey Ahead

In one organisation I replaced a project manager without the incumbent knowing that I'd been hired to replace her. The atmosphere was awkward to say the least.

I have to admit that she'd performed amazingly, as she had to manage a team where morale was low due to team losses. An immediate task was to reschedule a barrage of work. Central to her approach was to help both calm and stablise the team. Sadly, the project board was too focused on project timescales rather than the wellbeing of the team.

Often a project will take longer than originally planned. In addition, from the perspective of a project team member it can be difficult to understand the complexities of the road being travelled.

Selling the North Star

A classic example of outlining direction is to make it clear what the planning horizon or journey to the North Star will achieve. The latter is a term normally reserved for the following context: a company's vision for the future and a source of inspiration for all employees. It helps them understand what they are working towards and how their daily efforts contribute to a longer term goal.

From a programme/project perspective, let us consider the following distinction and use it as a way of encouraging or motivating team members.

Real World Case Study

A programme manager working on a building site constructing a community or cluster of houses was once asked about the difference between a project manager and a programme manager.

The Programme Manager pondered and then took a step ladder, wedging it into position we strode to the top making the following speech...

'Consider what we're doing today. Together, we're building new homes and we've got project managers assigned for each of the following areas: plumbing, construction, roofing, legal and electrics. Thank you for working so hard to achieve our goal. Do you know that in the distance I can see the new plot of land that I've negotiated for us to work on next? That's our future project and whilst working on that project we'll be renovating and integrating some of the existing buildings that are classified as heritage buildings. We'll be able to retain the existing external / frontage.'

The message was optimistic and if you consider projects such as the renovation of the East End of London and construction, use and repurposing of the Olympic Stadium and Athlete Village, these are examples of a shared and ultimately successful vision and achievement, respectively. The project statistics speak for themselves in terms of the teams that worked so hard to deliver: For example:

- 110,000 more jobs have been created across the host boroughs since 2012;
- Of the 70,000 London 2012 Games Makers, over 35,000 continue to volunteer in their communities; and
- 1 million+ people continue to visit the Olympic Park every year.

Example is Leadership

From a Project manager's perspective "Example is leadership" means that leadership is not just about giving orders or making decisions, but also about setting an example for others to follow. It suggests that the actions of a leader are more important than their words, and that a leader who demonstrates the desired behaviours will inspire others to follow suit.

If a leader wants their team to be honest and transparent, they should model these behaviours by being open and truthful in their communication. By doing so, they set a standard of honesty for their team and build trust and respect within the organisation.

Ultimately this creates a culture of excellence and inspires their team to achieve their full potential.

Peer based Learning contracts

In the past I've established mentoring systems. These have relied on the basis that both a mentor and mentee can learn from each other. One is not better or higher/lower than the other.

Formalising this through a learning contract that is confidential to the pairing or group can help track learning objectives and ways to demonstrate value attained.

These groupings can also forge trusted and confidential relationships, helping to drive personal excellence and self worth.

Learning contracts can include, for example:

- Timings to meet
- Coaching goals
- Shared project discussions (confidential)
- Shadowing to learn
- Forward / Rewind strategies to demonstrate learning
- A skills attainment list
- Progressive steps, for example stretch targets.

Such arrangements can also help to provide support against aggressive organisations and support anti-bullying and anti-mulling that can take place within an organisation.

Celebrating the success of Leavers!?

Sadly, I've worked for many organisations where if a project or departmental member resigns the line manager of that employee starts to treat him/her badly. It's almost as if they treat that resignation as betrayal!

Celebrating the success of a project team member is a great way to boost morale, increase motivation and strengthen team cohesion. When team members feel recognised and appreciated for their hard work and contributions, it can help build a positive and supportive work culture. This can, in turn, lead to better collaboration, increased engagement, and higher levels of productivity. It's also a way of, 'keeping the door open' for other opportunities. There are some management consultancy firms that establish alumni for leavers. One could cynically consider this as a future business prospecting ploy. I prefer to consider such an initiative as fostering a continuum of learning.

Celebrating success from a positive perspective celebrating the fact that a team member is moving to pastures new can help create a sense of accomplishment and pride among team members, which can lead to improved confidence. It's almost as if the team members helped to develop the leaver over time.

Let us hope that managers that feel betrayed can turn around their own attitude considering the need for facilitating a positive work culture, to boost both motivation and morale.

The Importance of Civility

The term "civility" comes from the Latin word "civilitas," which means "citizenship" or "civilization." Civility refers to the act of being respectful, courteous, and polite towards others. In the context of the workplace, civility means creating a positive and respectful work environment where everyone is treated with dignity and respect. A project manager who exhibits civility can create a positive work culture that promotes collaboration, productivity, and employee satisfaction. A project manager should show:

- Respect: to their team members by valuing their ideas and opinions.
- Empathy: towards their team members by understanding their concerns and challenges.
- Fairness: to all team members by providing equal opportunities and treating everyone with respect.
- Open communication: by encouraging open communication and being transparent with their team members.
- Positive attitude: by maintaining a positive attitude towards their team members and the project.
- Conflict resolution: by being skilled in conflict resolution to ensure that any disputes are resolved peacefully and fairly.

Performance orientated with perseverance

From a Project manager's perspective they have to sell an outward view of an optimist, building confidence in stakeholders and instilling belief in the team. "What does good look like" is a common phrase used in project management to help define expectations and success criteria.

Defining Deliverables

From a deliverable's perspective, we can use the example of a report or a site audit. With some project methodologies deliverables are also referred to as products. Their definition can include quality criteria, for example: Has the scope been signed off and even down to what will the content page look like from a titles perspective. Stakeholder agreement is essential considering if the report is a comprehensive, well-organised report together with the approval process being defined up front.

When setting expectations for project timelines, a project manager may ask the team to achieve tasks within an agreed timeline and budget, without cutting corners.

Stakeholder Engagement can also be considered from the context of an agreed Communication plan that includes frequency and format of updates.

For teams, good can be defined with competency frameworks, typically: do the team members collaborate effectively, resolve conflicts constructively and achieve against allocated check-point gates.

Retrospective Lens

From a Project manager's perspective they have to sell an outward view of an optimist, building confidence in stakeholders and instilling belief in the team. A retrospective lens is a way of looking at past events, experiences, and actions with the benefit of hindsight and a deeper understanding of their impact.

A Personal Growth Lens:

This involves considering past experiences and reflecting on what was learnt. The concept is that this can help you grow and develop as a person. For example, reflecting on a difficult project experience can help you identify patterns and aspects of the latter episode you want to avoid in the future. It's easier said than done!

A Project Organisation Learning Lens:

Conducting a retrospective review of a project or initiative can help an organisation identify what went well and what could be improved in future projects. For example, after completing a software development project, the project team can review their process and identify areas for improvement, such as more effective communication or better project management. Tools such as Jira can help set-up and vote on such aspects as the project progresses. Ideally, at set gates or every week between defined project sprints.

A Historical Analysis view point:

Examining past events from a retrospective lens can help us understand how they shaped the present. For example, looking back at historical events like the Civil Rights Movement or the Women's Suffrage Movement can help us appreciate the progress that has been made and identify areas where further progress is needed.

Creative Inspiration from others:

Reflecting on past experiences or art forms can inspire new ideas or artistic creations. For example, a filmmaker might draw inspiration from classic films or a writer might draw inspiration from the works of their favourite authors.

Valuing Diversity in your team can also help to drive new approaches and ways of working.

Trailblazing Evidence

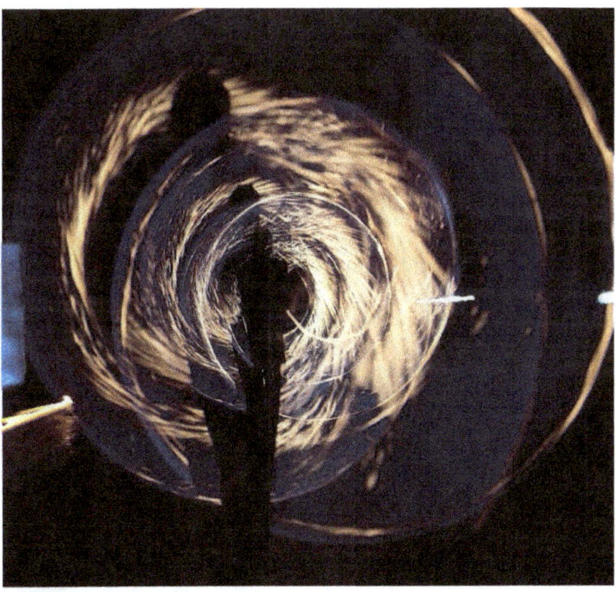

Here are 7 Guidance steps for improving the confidence that typically a governance structure of a project expects:

Guidance 1 - Practice makes perfect:

Rehearse your presentation to ensure that you are comfortable with your materials and know what you want to say. Be clear about your outcomes. Lobby for support even if this means a one to one session.

Guidance 2 - Know your audience:

Consider your audience's profile (power and influence), interest and knowledge level. Tailor your show and tell session with evidence to fit their needs and engage them in a meaningful way.

Guidance 3 - Keep it simple:

Make sure your session is simple, clear and easy to understand. Use simple language and avoid jargon or technical terms that may confuse your audience.

Guidance 4 - Use visuals:

Visual aids, such as posters, slides, or props, can help to illustrate your points and make your presentation more engaging.

Guidance 5 - Be enthusiastic:

Demonstrate your passion, this will help keep your audience interested in what you have to say.

Guidance 6 - Portray confident:

Speak clearly and confidently. Maintain eye contact with your audience and use a strong, clear voice.

Guidance 7 - Use Storytelling techniques:

Weave your presentation into a story that captures the audience's imagination. This supports making your presentation more memorable. Encourage audience participation by asking questions, inviting feedback, and encouraging discussio, generating greater interactivity

A Glossary that everyone can understand

Working on an integration project where multiple systems were required to exchange systems involved a number of Application Programming interfaces. It was hard for the 3rd parties and internal teams to get to grips with the terms and guiding principles of connectivity. One of the suppliers suggested an Interface catalogue where all integrations could move beyond a form field matrix.

OK, let's pause for a second... The language is getting complicated and the terms are very specific. The first place to start is to return to the original project objectives and position the required task so that everyone involved is aligned, from the delivery teams to the stakeholders. All must adopt a common language to facilitate common ground. This is also known as a taxonomy. Here are some general guidelines for its establishment.

Define the purpose of the taxonomy

Before creating a taxonomy, it is important to clearly define the purpose it will serve. This could be to organise data, improve search functionality, or standardise terminology.

Choose a relevant structure & naming conventions

Taxonomies can be hierarchical (with broad categories and subcategories) or faceted (with multiple dimensions or facets). Choose a structure that fits the nature of the project related content being classified and the needs of the users. The names of categories and subcategories should be clear, concise, and descriptive. They should also be consistent throughout the taxonomy to avoid confusion.

Test and refine a your project taxonomy

Once the taxonomy is created, it should be tested with users to ensure it is effective in meeting the defined purpose. Based on feedback, the taxonomy can be refined to improve usability and relevance.

It's also recommended to keep the associated taxonomy up-to-date, i.e: Taxonomies should be regularly reviewed and updated to ensure they remain relevant and accurate over time.

Overall, the key to using a taxonomy effectively is to have a clear understanding of its purpose, to choose a structure that fits the content and users' needs, and to continually test and refine the taxonomy to improve usability.

Real World Case study

Medical Surgeons use a Taxonomy to ensure that when everyone refers to a body part or particular procedure, consistency is achieved.

It is known as: Systematised Nomenclature of Medicine - Clinical Terms (SNOMED CT) to ensure consistency when referring to body parts, procedures, and other medical concepts.

SNOMED CT is a comprehensive and standardised clinical terminology that provides a common language for clinical documentation, communication, and analysis. It includes a hierarchical structure for organising medical concepts and relationships between them, allowing for precise and consistent representation of medical information across different healthcare settings and systems.

By using SNOMED CT, medical professionals can improve patient safety, reduce errors, and improve the quality of healthcare delivery.

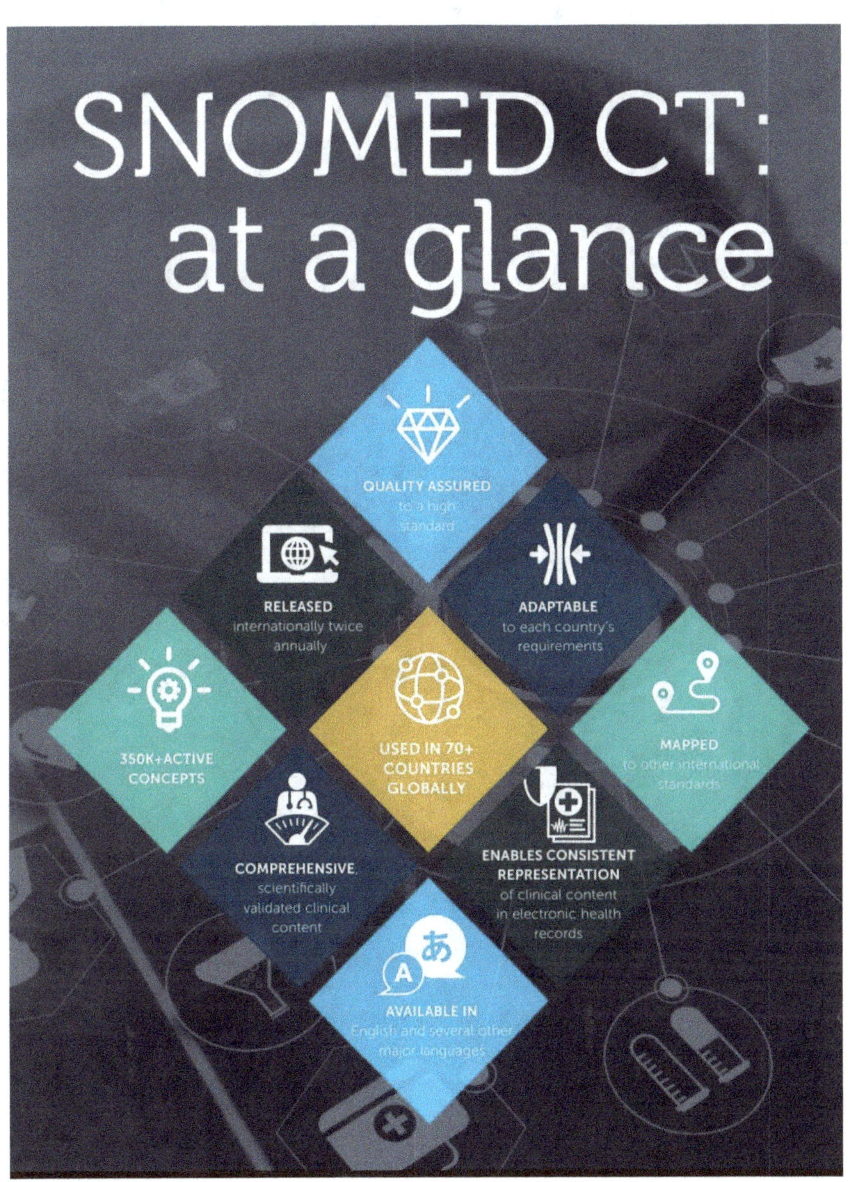
SNOMED CT:
at a glance
QUALITY ASSURED
to a high
standard
RELEASED
internationally twice
annually
ADAPTABLE
to each country's
requirements
350K+ACTIVE
CONCEPTS
USED IN 70+
COUNTRIES
GLOBALLY
MAPPED
to other international
standards
COMPREHENSIVE,
scientifically
validated clinical
content
ENABLES CONSISTENT
REPRESENTATION
of clinical content
in electronic health
records
あ
A
AVAILABLE IN
English and several other
major languages

Adaptive to the change challenge ahead

During my PhD I worked on the concept of understanding what strategies could be developed to align the constant progression of business technology and how a firm evolves throughout their life. Interestingly I noted that the ice age took place approximately 2.6 million years ago to 11,700 years ago. Much of the Earth's surface was covered in ice, resulting in significant changes to the climate, vegetation, and animal populations. Some species taking a sense and respond approach to environmental change survived. Some species thrived during the ice age, while others were unable to adapt and became extinct.

Change Methods

For example, during the last glacial maximum, which occurred around 20,000 years ago, many large mammal species in North America, such as woolly mammoths and sabre-toothed cats, became extinct, while smaller mammals such as rodents and shrews were able to survive.

Some of the ways that species have adapted to changes caused by the ice age include changes in diet, migration to new areas, changes in body size and shape, and changes in behaviour. For example, some species of birds and butterflies have shifted their ranges northward in response to changes in temperature, while some mammals have adapted to cold temperatures by growing thicker fur or changing their metabolism.

Overall, the ice age was a time of significant change for the Earth's ecosystems, and many species were able to adapt and evolve in response to these changes.

Change Impact Analysis Grids

Many organisations develop a change impact analysis grid. This valuable tool helps us understand, document and get agreement on a , 'as is' state and highlight what needs to be done to achieve a, 'to be' state. It promotes proactive risk management, enhances communication and collaboration, and supports effective decision-making.

In addition, by assessing the potential impacts of a change, a project team can take steps to minimise disruption to the project or organisation. This includes planning for contingencies and developing a phased approach to the change.

Typically, at a change board the project manager needs to attend and present a coherent case for the change, including in advance agreement to mitigate typically and out of hours agreed downtime. For example, access to buildings, systems (including data) and logistics (fulfilment channels).

Sense and Respond

In order to sense and respond to change and hence survive, it's essential to categorise and link the cultural make-up of both technical and business divisions of an enterprise from the perspective of the:

- Relationship between employees and their attitude to authority
- Consideration of the variance in the way project members think and learning,

- Attitudes to people & teams (To and through an organisation)
- Accomodation / Capability of speed to change / responding to an environmental
- Latter includes partner or 3rd party management.
- Changing or transforming an organisation suit its culture
- Ways / methods of motivating and rewarding team members,
- Methods used to critically review and manage conflict resolution

The following diagram developed by Dr Savi shows an alignment model that could work for projects.

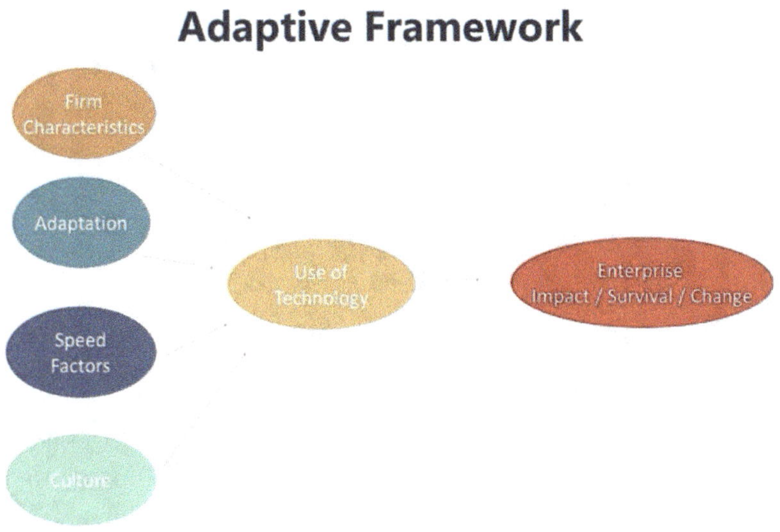

Adaptive Framework

Firm Characteristics

Adaptation

Use of Technology

Enterprise Impact / Survival / Change

Speed Factors

Culture

Gamification of Change:

Gamification is another way of understanding the impact of change.

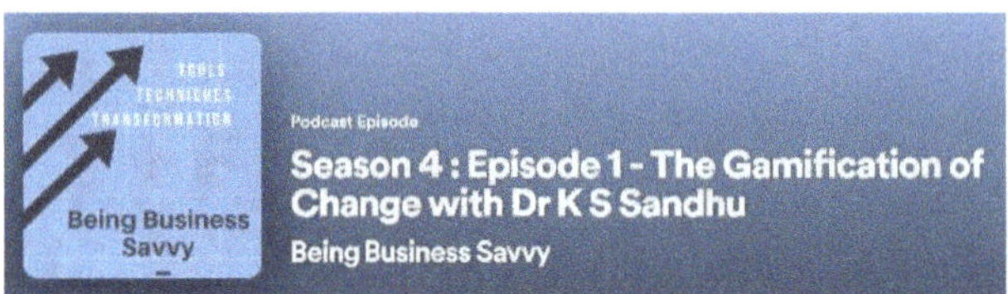

In an in depth interview between the author and Dr K S Sandhu, he (Dr Sandhu) reveals his pioneering virtual software where groups (Stakeholders) can come together to experience risk free simulations. Learn more via the Being Business Savvy Podcast, Season 4, Episode 1 - The Gamification of Change.

Navigate the Stars

In an earlier chapter we defined the use of North Star planning, especially for focusing team members on a vision for joint success.

As a creative project manager, you can use tools to help understand where you are on your project journey. Making time for check-points to assure previous markers are showing up - just like anchored water buoys.

The most common kind of water buoy markers are lateral or channel buoys. Lateral buoys are channel markers indicating the sides of a navigable channel; you can avoid sand bars and other hazards by keeping within the markers.

Buoys are anchored to the seabed. In some places, buoys may be posts or sticks in the ground. Generally, where bigger ships go, bigger buoyage is used. As you head into less populated or shallower areas the marks will reduce in size until you finally meet withies (sticks in the ground usually made of willow).

Interestingly, from a Star Trek Next Generation (TNG) reference, Buoys could also be used as sensor devices in a way similar to mobile probes. In a fictional instance during the year 2370 these devices were set-up as a security measure as Federation (Star Fleet) established a series of checkpoints and sensor buoys along their border with Cardassian (another fictional alien race) space. (For more detail see TNG: "Pre-emptive Strike").

The Trouble with Project Charter

Back to the point about navigating one's way through a project. Sure, a project charter can authorise the start of a project and provides the project manager with the authority to allocate resources and carry out the work required to achieve the project objectives. It is also usually developed during the initiation phase of a project and serves as a reference for the project team, stakeholders and sponsors throughout the project lifecycle.

Although a project charter is critical to the success of a project, it may not provide an adequate framework for navigating potential risks, for example, limited risk assessment, lack of or poor mitigation strategies and inadequate contingency planning, i.e: The project team may need to conduct a more in-depth risk assessment, develop a comprehensive risk management plan and create contingency plans to address unforeseen events that could impact the project's success.

Communicate To collaboration

When you read more into the quote it reveals itself to be true. Often we forget about the need to respect that different people have different ways in how they communicate and feel both safe and respected. For example, in the early days of Twitter an educator was using post lecture direct messaging to capture questions from shy attendees.

Collaboration is Key : Be Highly communicative

Collaboration should be viewed as a helpful tool for achieving certain goals, rather than an absolute requirement for all tasks and activities.

In other words, while collaboration can be very effective for certain types of work, it's not always necessary or practical for every situation. Individuals and teams should be empowered to use collaboration as a tool when it makes sense for their specific needs and goals.

Is collaboration a tool or a rule? This idea has been expressed by various people in different contexts.

For example, in his book "The Culture Code: The Secrets of Highly Successful Groups," author Daniel Coyle writes about the importance of creating a culture where collaboration is encouraged but not forced. He emphasises that collaboration should be seen as a tool that can be used when it's most effective, rather than a mandatory requirement for all tasks.

In the context of project management, the idea of "collaboration over process" has become popular in recent years. This approach emphasises the importance of collaboration between team members, but also recognises that there are times when a more structured approach may be necessary.

A Framework for Project Retrospective Sessions.

Overall, the concept of "collaboration as a tool, not a rule" reflects the idea that collaboration should be seen as a valuable resource that can be used strategically, rather than an absolute requirement for all situations.

Agile based retrospective sessions both during and at the end of a project can provide useful input to further stages and new phases. Essentially, taking a positive approach:

- What went well,
- What could we do better and
- What will we achieve or improve the next time we meet?

Here are some fresh ideas for achieving a constructive, rather than critical retrospective - based on collating a range of new ideas.

- **Glad, Sad and Mad:**
  Classifying issues in these categories
- **Lean Coffee:**
  On the spot chats to push forward away from blockers
- **The 4 Ls:**
  This approach helps you to discover what your team **liked, learned, lacked, and longed for.**
- **Turn that Ship around! A Gamification Example:**
  Asking a team to draw sails and anchors to represent what is holding them back.

Lobbying in a difficult project situation

This can be a challenging task, but the good news is that there are a number of routes to consider:

Build relationships: with stakeholders and decision-makers

By taking time to consider / understand their perspectives, needs and concerns. Ideally, consider opportunities to collaborate and build their trust. That you can deliver. You can showcase some aspects of a solution. Mock-up or draw a vision chart to 'sell' the final outcome. Show and Tells are popular but pitch them based on the audience. Make the latter graphically appealing and don't be afraid to make the concept simple but not too patronising!

Effective communication is key to successful lobbying

Articulate your goals, concerns and ideas, and make sure to listen actively to others' perspectives as well. Use data and evidence to support your suppositions whenever possible.

Develop a strong / compelling view

Have a clear and compelling perspective that you will articulate. Be persistent but not too pushy: Lobbying in a difficult project situation may require persistence but you need to test the waters first. Ideally, before an important meeting, for example: a strategic board session, ensure you spend time with key decision makers either in segmented smaller group settings or one to one sessions - Remember to not do this at the last minute but with plenty of time scheduled.

Search / Find Suitable allies

Look for others who share your goals and concerns and work to build a coalition of support. This can help you amplify your message and make it more likely that decision-makers will listen to your ideas. Get the allies to preach your message by subtle pre-rehearsed prompts.

Frame your ideas in terms of shared goals and objectives:

Highlight areas where your proposals can benefit multiple parties. Overall, as a creative project manager you will need a good combination of communication skills, relationship-building, persistence and strategic thinking.

Taking a thoughtful and proactive approach, you can increase your chances of success and help move a project forward in a positive direction or desired outcome.

Avoid being a victim of Bullying!

You may be asking yourself why the context of bullying and even mulling (collective bullying) is being considered. As this book outlines real world examples to learn from, here's one that will get you to appreciate why.

Real world Case Study

A few years ago at a Project definition workshop at the Department of Health a one day session was being held to determine requirements for a patient record system that would follow a patient from their General Practice surgery to treatment throughout their life.

Sadly, with limited time outs and a total of 30 attendees comprising the facilitating lead management consultants, clinical specialists and supplier representatives, it was an exhaustive day.

After the session I was approached by a clinical specialist that was shy and quietly spoken. She stated that during the session her opinion was overlooked a number of times, when she attempted to interact or raise a point. At times she felt that the suppliers present were overriding or steering the meeting in a non-consensus direction - describing the outcome as being not customer centric.

The lesson here is to know your audience and find alternative ways to capture participation and acknowledge respectively the needs of your true end client to achieve mutual satisfaction. Asking from the start of a meeting, 'what does good look like?'

The organisers could have organised on the day checkpoints, summary sessions, break out rooms, post workshop surveys and yellow post it categorisation methods to consolidate ideas into logical groupings.

Technically briefed and reliance on realistic options.

Can a Project manager that manages construction projects also manage an information technology, say communications infrastructure project? My view is that it would be hard. However, foundations can be learnt and reliance on solution clarity can help support him/her. In terms of if the quality of the project would be the same for each sector? It's unlikely!

Presenting Feasible Options

Here are seven recommended steps to help define, assess and articulate a solution.

Step 1: Understand the problem at hand - This helps for all goals to be open and transparent.

Step 2: Gather / Collect data about the problem - This can help identify potential solutions and evaluate their feasibility.

Step 3: Brainstorm Solutions via organised / structured workshops - Ensure the inclusion of documented 1-to-1 sessions. From these sessions generate a list of potential solutions (include impossible dreams!).

Throughout all sessions establish from the outset open communication and collaboration. Use technology to summarise, document and include the participation and contribution of virtual members.

Step 4: Evaluate Options - Review the list of potential solutions and evaluate their feasibility based on several factors such as cost, time, resources, and impact on the project's objectives. Consider solution reliability and resilience. Most importantly, assign a quality assessment against each of these items. Some organisation like the drawing up of grids and mapped financial implications against each option.

Steps 4 and 5: Prioritise and Present solutions - Use a change impact grid to help assess your 'as is' and 'to be' state. Prioritise the feasible solutions based on their potential impact, feasibility, and resource availability. Present Options: Present the feasible solutions to the project stakeholders. Use visuals such as graphs, charts and diagrams to illustrate the potential solutions. T-shirt sizing a solution can help to simplify your final options together with getting subject matter experts to draw and share current processes so that no subtlety or hidden sub-systems are missed.

Step 6: Solicit Feedback - Allow stakeholders to provide feedback on the options presented - Listen to their concerns, suggestions and ideas.

Step 7: Make a Decision- Based on the feedback received, make a decision on which solution to pursue. Communicate the decision to the team and stakeholders.

In summary, presenting feasible options requires careful planning, collaboration, and effective communication. By following these steps outlined in this chapter, a project leader can present viable options to stakeholders and make an informed decision on the best course of action for the project.

Simplification

One of the first exercises I was asked to perform when I first started my PhD was to explain to my research supervisor the difference between an analogy and a metaphor.

Interestingly, they are both figures of speech used to make a comparison between two things. However, there is a subtle difference between the two.

An analogy is a comparison between two things that are different in some ways but have similar characteristics or features. It often involves explaining something complex by using a simpler or more familiar concept. For example, "The human brain is like a computer. Just as a computer processes information, the brain processes thoughts and memories."

A metaphor, on the other hand, is a figure of speech that directly compares two things by stating that one thing is another thing. It is a way of describing something by using a word or phrase that is not meant to be taken literally. For example, "He is a shining star" compares a person to a star, suggesting that he is bright, talented, or successful.

In summary, while both analogy and metaphor are used to make a comparison, an analogy compares two things that are different but share some similarities, while a metaphor equates two things that are not the same, highlighting a similarity or shared characteristic between them.

How do we use Simplification techniques in projects?

Sometimes explaining basic concepts for deliverables and key project objectives to stakeholders can be hard as it can be misconstrued and perceived as patronising. The guiding principle must be patience, respect and appropriateness in terms of timing and delivery method. Sure, show and tell sessions during a project can be scheduled but if a stakeholder is still exhibiting signs of confusion, then the latter verbal / language techniques can be used when explaining concepts. Simplifying customer journeys, concepts, ideas and roadmaps can often be achieved through the use of storyboarding or sketching workflows, known as swimlanes together with cause and effect fishbone diagrams.

The examples below show how characters can be established with dialogues and narratives to help outline core principles and expected outcomes.

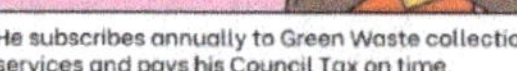
He subscribes annually to Green Waste collection services and pays his Council Tax on time.

We currently rely on taking payments over the phone by noting personal details.

The council will guide you through a new way to pay for a range of services

To develop an Automated Payment system that each department affected will transfer our residents to when they are ready to pay

Payments are receipted, filed by our department and we can carry on offering you our services

Creativity warning!

A creativity warning of the use of this approach is based on the need to always appreciate the culture of a firm.

For example, if you've worked hard to develop an explainer video and the organisation are resist to its use (probably because they either don't have a strong technical infrastructure or don't consider video as an appropriate way to impart information efficiently), the perception could be that too much time is being spent on content vs project commitment! i.e: Some stakeholders may consider this as being a waste of resources and time, instead of focusing against a backdrop of a tight schedule.

During the development of these tools it is best to trial and also consider the concept of lobbying for its use and eventual adoption.

Sometimes developing an idea and a partial build can help to 'test the waters'. This can help gain buy-in to the investment of its potential usefulness.

What we leave behind

When the streets are empty after your welcome home parade from Space. If all that remains is just trails of ticker tape on the floor, someone will need to tidy up. That tidy up will involve project closure documentation and an official approved exit procedure for your project and team. There will also be memories of the impact you had on others. I often ask the question what makes a builder or project manager want or wish to move on to his/her next project or pursuit? Is it just the joy of being in the moment of delivery? In this chapter we discover a few possible reasons.

Financial gain and Creative Fulfilment

Project managers may be motivated by financial gain and may want to move on to a new project that offers a higher profit margin or a bigger payout. They also may have a desire to create something new and innovative, and may want to move on to a new project that challenges them creatively.

Personal satisfaction

Returning to the theme of being in the moment, Project Managers may derive personal satisfaction from completing a project, and may want to move on to a new project to experience that sense of accomplishment again.

Career advancement

Different Project managers could be in a variety of career positions and they may be motivated by career advancement and may wish to take on bigger, more complex projects to showcase their skills and expertise.

Market demand

Is another driver with the motivation being to pursue projects that are in high demand or have the potential for significant growth. Ultimately, the reasons why a project manager or builder may want to move on and pursue their next project depends on their individual motivations, goals, and priorities.

The nature of the role is the real driver

In Toy Story the character Buzz Lightyear is challenged about who he is. His answer is simply:

> *Excuse me, I think the word you're searching for is 'Space Ranger' - Buzz Lightyear (Toy Story 1)*

Let us explore another motivation for moving from project to project in a bold and confident way. Maybe it's the role itself that is the driver. A project manager has great power and in the words of Stan Lee: 'With great power comes great responsibility'.

Where else can a multitude of attributes assemble, align and assure success for the challenge ahead. The Project manager has the unique position to influence and lead his/her team towards a successful launch and descent to a perfect landing. With analytics, operational excellence to deliver at the end he/she defines, sells and achieves a quality delivery throughout all the stages presented, negotiated and awarded.

In this book the author is your Avenger, providing you with enhancements to your already worthy super powers, to be heroic in all you do and win for others not just for yourself...

Epilogue

At the start of this book I gave the analogy of Captain Kirk asking Scotty, the starship Enterprise's chief engineer, of how long it would take Engineering (Scotty's department) to get out of an impending disaster. Typically, requesting more power.

Captain Kirk: "Scotty, we need more power!"
Scotty: "Captain, I'm giving her all we got!"

Captain Kirk can be considered as the client or the ultimate highest level of stakeholder with engineers being the teams that have to deliver a commitment undertaken. Kirk in this case is not interested in the detail, the process or challenges it will take to 'turn up the dial'. Sound familiar?

By applying a variety of techniques to anticipate problems (plan) and solve post implementation issues from the outset of a project, creative Project Managers can deliver a continuum of empowerment and positive outcomes.

Closing with another Star Trek quote from Captain Kirk:

"You know the greatest danger facing us is ourselves, an irrational fear of the unknown. But there's no such thing as the unknown - only things temporarily hidden, temporarily not understood."

THANKS AGAIN FOR ALL YOUR SUPPORT AND KEEP ON KEEPING ON!

Acknowledgement

My experience is based on the delivering real world projects and consider that life is a journey, with an aim to learn and support others on route.

Personal Thanks to my editors: Ian Gordon, Rishem Khattar & Rohin S Arora

I'm also appreciative to all the creative souls I've meet and to all those who continue to light the way to discover new pathways for both project and personal success.

About The Author

Dr Savi Arora

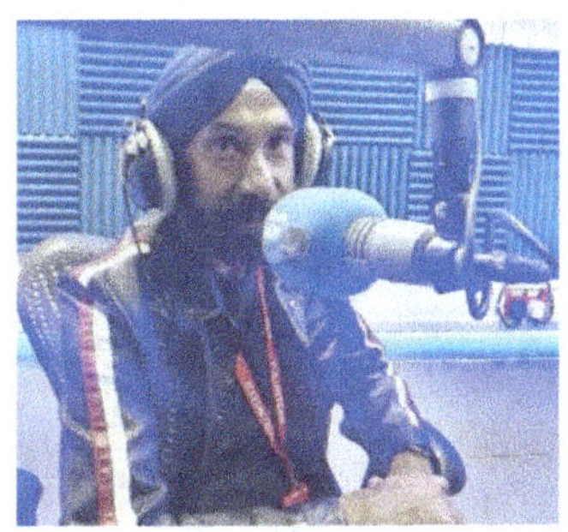

Dr Savi is a renown web strategist & accomplished Program Director. He's written several books and articles on best practice in areas such as Project Management and Creative Techniques. With over 40 years of experience as a company program Director working at Computacenter, Vodafone, O2, Microsoft, Sky TV, Next PLC and Honda. He has a Postgraduate in Management, MBA and PhD.

Dr Savi has worked on Sky.com/shop, O2 Priority Moments, NHS national eLearning rollout, the first apps via 3, MyVodafone App and Honda Marine, just to mention a few.

His approach has always been to build on measured phased approach with an understanding of business continuity and longevity from the outset. His motto is to realise success for all.

thoughts

Afterword & One last Thing...

If you enjoyed this book or found it useful, I'd be very grateful if you'd post a short review on Amazon. Your support really does make a difference and I will read all the reviews personally so I can get your feedback and make this book even better.

Further reading:

"The Creative Habit" by Twyla Tharp
"The Art of Possibility" by Rosamund Stone Zander and Benjamin Zander
"Managing the Design Process-Concept Development" by Terry Lee Stone
"Designing Your Life" by Bill Burnett and Dave Evans
"The Lean Startup" by Eric Ries
"The Art of Creative Thinking" by Rod Judkins
"Design Thinking" by Tim Brown
"The Power of Intentional Leadership" by Anil K. Gupta
"How to Make Ideas Happen" by Scott Belsky
"The Innovator's Dilemma" by Clayton Christensen
"Managing Creative People" by Gordon Torr
"Designing for Growth" by Jeanne Liedtka and Tim Ogilvie
"Creativity, Inc." by Ed Catmull
"The Art of Project Management" by Scott Berkun
"The War of Art" by Steven Pressfield
"The Design of Everyday Things" by Don Norman
"The Elements of User Experience" by Jesse James Garrett
"Thinking, Fast and Slow" by Daniel Kahneman
"Creative Confidence" by Tom Kelley and David Kelley
"The 7 Habits of Highly Effective People" by Stephen Covey
"The Art of Strategy" by Avinash K. Dixit and Barry J. Nalebuff
"The Innovator's Solution" by Clayton Christensen and Michael E. Raynor
"The Practice" by Seth Godin
"Drive: The Surprising Truth About What Motivates Us" by Daniel H. Pink
"The Art of Possibility" by Rosamund Stone Zander and Benjamin Zander
"Creative Strategy and the Business of Design" by Douglas Davis
"The Checklist Manifesto" by Atul Gawande
"The Lean Product Playbook" by Dan Olsen
"Change by Design" by Tim Brown
"The Lean UX" by Jeff Gothelf
"The Art of Explanation" by Lee LeFever
"The Design Thinking Playbook" by Michael Lewrick, Patrick Link, and Larry Leifer

"The Lean Enterprise" by Jez Humble, Joanne Molesky, and Barry O'Reilly
"Sprint: How to Solve Big Problems and Test New Ideas in Just Five Days" by Jake Knapp, John Zeratsky, and Braden Kowitz
"The Innovator's DNA" by Clayton Christensen, Jeff Dyer, and Hal Gregersen
"The Art of Client Service" by Robert Solomon
"Articulating Design Decisions" by Tom Greever
"The Four Steps to the Epiphany" by Steve Blank
"The Business Model Canvas" by Alexander Osterwalder and Yves Pigneur
"The Experience Economy" by Joseph Pine and James Gilmore
"The Art of Explanation" by Lee LeFever
"The Little Book of Design Research Ethics" by Caroline Jarrett and Mark

www.ingramcontent.com/pod-product-compliance
Lightning Source LLC
Chambersburg PA
CBHW071044220526
45467CB00004B/1671

* 9 7 9 8 3 9 0 9 7 1 6 8 0 *